Man at Leisure

Alexander Trocchi

ONEWORLD
CLASSICS

ONEWORLD CLASSICS LTD
London House
243-253 Lower Mortlake Road
Richmond
Surrey TW9 2LL
United Kingdom
www.oneworldclassics.com

Man at Leisure first published in 1972
This edition first published by Oneworld Classics Limited in 2009
Reprinted 2011

© The Estate of Alexander Trocchi 1972

Front cover image © Georges Noblet

Printed in Great Britain by MPG Books Group

ISBN: 978-1-84749-100-8

Contents

Preface

ALTHOUGH HE IS STILL LARGELY IGNORED by the staider organs of literary reference, as he was in his lifetime by most of the establishment of the day, Alexander Trocchi remains one of the most interesting, if controversial, writers of his time, still much read, and not only in the Scotland of his birth, where he is widely admired by younger writers. He is the British equivalent of the American beats, but the tradition to which he belongs is really more that of the "damned" French writers, from Baudelaire and Rimbaud to Céline and Genet. One could almost also mention Cocteau, who was responsible for introducing him to heroin, the cause of his eventual downfall and death. It was responsible for his short career as a novelist: after the Fifties he could only concentrate on shorter work, such as articles, stories, translations handed in a few pages at a time and, of course, poetry.

If this collection of his poems, republished after three and a half decades, seems to vary enormously in content, style and use of language, it is because they were written over a twenty-year period from his leaving Glasgow in 1951 up to first publication in 1972, when it was only by obtaining unauthorized entry to his flat and desk drawers that I got hold of the manuscript. The book had been contracted, but Trocchi kept on avoiding delivery on various pretexts. As a result I had to edit poems that the author had little looked at, and in some cases had to revise and finish them. Otherwise they would never have been published or perhaps would have been sold to another publisher, because Alex, always in desperate need of money, had no scruples about selling the same manuscript to as many different publishers as would sign contracts.

Abbreviations might have been extended, lines rewritten in other ways, orthography changed, had the author been willing to find the time to rework his poems in my presence, but he accepted the *fait accompli* with good grace. As I have said elsewhere, heroin addiction might give its victim inspiring ideas, but it takes away the ability to concentrate on serious creative work. Nevertheless, this, Trocchi's only surviving collection of poems, although rough in many ways, is revealing about his background of literary knowledge, and often lyrical in its total lack of inhibition, anticipating the greater literary freedom that was already following the censorship trials of the Sixties, which included his own work.

This volume keeps the original introduction by William Burroughs, whom he met through me, an event that resulted in them becoming good friends. Perhaps some of Burroughs' influence can be detected in some of the later work, which is fragmented in ways that often resemble the writings of the early surrealists. This is very appropriate, because Trocchi's life was a surreal one, and the obvious genuine literary talent that went into his best work now seems certain to endure as a significant part of twentieth-century literature.

– John Calder
April 2009

Introduction

"Alex Trocchi Cosmonaut of Inner Space"

I T WAS AT THE 1962 WRITER'S CONFERENCE in Edinburgh that I first heard Alex describe himself in these terms. He was standing in front of a large audience and said, after a pause in which he seemed to be at a loss for words:

"I am a cosmonaut of inner space."

Alex is a forceful and decisive public speaker and his pauses are worth waiting for. This conference, organized by John Calder, established the books that had grown out of the underground culture as literature and the writers of these books as important literary figures.

The poems in this book are reminiscent of John Donne and the metaphysical poets, and I had already described Alex as a modern metaphysical poet before I came across his poem to John Donne. Alex writes about spirit, flesh and death and the vision that comes through the flesh... "Somewhere between Nice and Monte Carlo and must depart soon in beds, fields, cinemas or pigsties centuries of rock laugh white teeth at death in a brown land children play dirty in marketplaces crunching sugar skulls cats laugh their pointed teeth from the wet streets a boy's cry over the city".

"My personal Ides," he said.

Wrote at night red ink on cheap paper

"I wonder when a woman will walk naked to me?"

Chalk marks on a wall in a black cave

Ob scene

Ab sent

Shut the lavatory door and lock it like he was hot see?

The Milky Way whips my sperm to the sky starship text book for today warm blood snake thrust pure salt visibility excellent on what fantastic world in the desert distances are not far not a whisper of a tent plague above the city and the weapons of war are perished. Fuck. Good luck.

Perhaps writers are actually *readers* from hidden books. These books are carefully concealed and surrounded by deadly snares. It is a dangerous expedition to find one of these books and bring back a few words. Genet said of a Catholic pederast who shall be nameless here "*Il n'a pas le courage d'être écrivain*".

Alex has this courage so essential to a writer. He has been there and has read what he writes.

I remember reading *Cain's Book* for the first time: the barge the dropper the heroin you can feel it or see it. He has been there and brought it back. Many writers when they start to write withdraw from the source of their writing, but Alex has not done this and if his life may have taken time from his work it gives back a rare vitality. The poems in this book are buoyant with that vitality and the hope which is so much a part of Alex's personality. One always feels better after seeing Alex and that is indeed a precious gift, a quality that has brought to his door hundreds of young people over the years. Alex has been for them the focal point in the underground literary scene which he pioneered with *Cain's Book*. He has come a long way since then. One hopes that his long boat will turn into a long book about that trip through inner and outer space.

– William S. Burroughs
April 1972

Man at Leisure

Where to Begin

Where to begin
which sin
under what sun
what work begun
or play
the day
or night away?

Myrtle with the Light Blue Hair

I was like she was, hot, see?
a fat, lovable little boy
with an eye that peeped at her, what she
showed the toad, & not coy...
the slicks, flats, elastic tensions
of her great, her imperial thighs,
the torque of her hot delta which
smoked a turkish cigarette
for me to see that she
was all lips and hips
at the green pod she burgeoned downwards from
like a butter bean.

then, her belly dangling
like an egg on poach
she scissored her legs cleverlie
and spat out the roach,
which... I raised to my lips

I was like she was and she at her ease
& ripe was she
as a thumbpress on a camembert cheese
her chevron gamey-dark, like good game
as she came on me
& retrieved her cigarette,
inhaled, & threw it away...
collecting me to her like a windy skirt
before she leaned against me, like a sea.

Bubonics

1

Poetry is a wordy suppuration
often indelicate, like hate;
which came into being after the Fall
before which, all
expression was written in hot flanks
effectively. Thanks
to that, there was no call
for spiritual menstruation...

2

Literature is that body of doctrine
whose carnality is metaphorical
whose pretension is categorical
and which, incidentally
is worth bugger-all...

3

Love (what mothers call infatuation)
is a cosmic vibration
often immoderate
like hate;
it lives in the thighs
is consummate
in beds, fields, cinemas or pigsties
according to mood, heat & uphertunicky...

5

The Water Spout

It is evening. The flat sea
draws in its edges from the serrated coast.
One's voice is lost, well-lost
down here in the Midi
hanging, a ridiculously silent cannon
on a promontory
somewhere between Nice and Monte Carlo.

Nothing but water from the waterspout.
The glad brown bodies of the women gone
to winter places, winter loves
to crunch dry toasts, discuss
winter situations. And I
who arrived too late
and must depart soon
listen to the water from the waterspout
somewhere between Nice and Monte Carlo.

Wind from the Bosphorus

Tzigane
late of the Bosphorus
come through the stink of many nations
on a painted cart
to water himself
his brown-thighed woman
brats
his bowlegged knackery
in the mauve bole of Paris.

in Greece
he got one child and syphilis
discreetly, of a blonde Roumanian tart
who (torn in her shy soul)
spent half her time being a refugee, the other
half
bucking for dear life
under the swarthy weight of sailors.

a young man
stalking a butterfly
found a flare-red skirt, a high-cheeked
gypsywoman
and lay with her behind a bush in adultery
caught
still supine, the winds of the East
and of Roumanian Anna

later
he carried with him
more than a gypsy's fading heat, but was not
much concerned
desire being international, of more significance

than the incidental *cum multis aliis*
he carried to the clinic
where
he was treated
by more civilised persons who showed
little interest
in what they called (with an utter lack of
sensibility)
"the source of infection"
as though
nothing else had been carried to him from the East
on the wind of her body.

Sad' Poems

> "He's got one? A chimpanzee?
> Whatever for? To furnish his
> bestiary withal."
>
> *The Cock of the Walk*
> Marquis de Sade

Monasts
do not have to be
pederasts
rumination
an accumulation
of pasts
and last week's telecasts

Baron Lust's last list
cast
doubt
on the cost
of toast
on the coast
of Cap d'Ail

Cops at the Cap
clear cunts from the map
and keep the Coast clear
for arseholes on the mere.

"Unless She Comes"

Unless she comes
will be no end to waiting
and night xtinguishes
unless she comes

Unless she comes
the cutting shutter falls
in void unanswered calls
unless she comes

Unless she comes
my soul in grief collide
a little death have died
unless she comes

Unless she comes
with dawn my heart will crack
I'll know she won't be back
& now will never come

The Brown Land

the brown land does not resent stone faces
nor faces of flesh, the serape
weaves broad time in many colours
death in the brown tree—
is a skull death? the murmur of bone?
what prayer is answered by the gods at Yucatan?

centuries of rock, of brown women
laugh white teeth at death
in a brown land, children play
at sun, dirty in marketplaces
crunching sugar skulls.

the brown women have brown breasts and brown loins
they mock death in brown wombs
a new cell, *casamiento*! the brown land
does not resent its brown women
the brown women are water in a brown land.

and brown girls will be brown mothers
with brown bellies more fruitful than brown land
laugh at death, a red dance
before our Virgin at Guadeloupe.
eternity has been struck at Teotihuacan...

Portrait

as night fell
sans paramour
and spoordrawn into dance
he came to the city
city of obelisk
and risk
tambourine, turkspleasure
swarthy muleteer
the abominable Berthe
à plat ventre
(they say she will have none of any other position)

he drank
vin blanc
in the Café of the Two Hemispheres
ignored
the Sisters of Mercy
the gentle supplication
of the peanut vendor
the vendor of lotteries
and
loth to offend her
told
the abominable Berthe
a plain untruth
about his condition

not held
by the gay synopsis
of murder
the little red Calvary in the third column
(the paper bored him
humanists bred him

logic cured him)
he ordered oysters
—a broken acrobat, a strangled nude
possibly one of the Merciful Sisters
—and counted the shells

the café spread
a helio lance
in the hollow ingot
of his isolation
(the oysters were no consolation)
truthfully
he would have settled for something rather less than
a woman of the Ptolemies.

Poem

Who will break a boy's cry over the city?
suddenly,
taken in the dim treachery of walls
a hand all bone moving spiderpinkly
at seek,
setting feet stealthily in the ribs of the garden?

Who will cast a boy's flesh over the city?
whitely,
uttering deprecations
a tongue, all stone, muttering
at fall,
like toppling brick in the ribs of the garden?

Who will shake a boy's hairs over the city?
secretly,
lipping black feathers, stir
thighs alone, a cat obliquely
at wait,
the eyes of an owl in the ribs of the garden?

Who will pluck a boy's eyes over the city?
dumbly,
counting pale skulls
who will atone in the graveyard
at prayer,
speak beads in the ribs of the garden?

Who will stab a boy's heart over the city?
sadly,
and cry with his own
to be at one with his god
at judgement,
deals death in the ribs of the garden...?

He Tasted History with a Yellow Tooth

the long tusktooth of his nether jaw
cast a yellow shadow
broke through the thin bone of history
loosing tides.
"my personal ides"
he said, wrote at night
red ink on cheap paper
his big quick letters (always for the greater glory of God)
round as nuts or girlbreasts
a terrible child's message to a world at war.

eggs again.
my aunt laid an egg once, all smooth and creamy
you wanted to stroke it as you want to stroke a woman
but she was ashamed of it
and took it away from me.
I think she buried it in the garden—
anyway, there's a patch of violets there
ten yards from the stair
that goes to the loft where my uncle kept the saddles
and they bleed each spring,
in spring there is a bleeding.

he's a bit of a Jesuit
his brain full of bits of history
which he chews over with his yellow tooth,
a strange Balkan name, an Icelandic God,
did you know that somewhere in Africa
a woman walks naked to her wedding?

I tell you there is no use talking about the "Renaissance"
it was a falling off, a *ruining*
of towers (you know the derivation?)
Late? I suppose it is. Not want tea?
—I wonder when a woman will walk naked to me?

In the White Bowl of Yr Thighs

In the white bowl of yr thighs
a dead man lies
minutely quivering, my dear
as does an oar's
blade water.
The seething mice
that nested there
as he did core thee!

In the white bowl of yr thighs
my red cherry lies
my needles knit
small birds atwit
in yr groin's great grab
and shuddering tomtit?

Ding dong dell
pussy's in the well
yr white thighs' bowl
Val de Grâce
chalk marks on a wall.

Love Poem

Her commands
commend themselves to men
    their glands
...a liquid magic moves
as under winds do sands
stretch timeless shelves
    in dunes
on which a red sun bled
through net, the trap in trees
    on ground
shifts faerie coins
faint cosmic runes
and there the same gold ball
    aglint on ground
like diamond sands
    while I
from out amongst her loins
my lips across the pale expanse
    of abdomen
    am hugely drawn
on the breath of my body's loam.

Belinda

In the black cave
of her delight
where moon is
is always night;
on oiled bellies
sun is bright

It is punday, funday
in the golden caravan,
and in the caravan of her night
she feeds her milk to mouthing man

It is sunday
and her tits are tight
for lips to be against
her belly ripe with mouthing man

+

When machines
make beans
and men and women
on Monday afternoons
in all the towns
and fields, in all the lanes,
and in the barns
and on the beaches
and on the beds
and on Tuesday morning's agenda
I shall ever surrender
to gold-bellied Belinda

Obscene

I

Ob scene
Ob es   (Ob eys
Ob est   A pest)
Ob sessus
Ob estis   (Abscesses)
Ab sent.

II

Obscenity is a purse
in your own pocket

Don't look at me
and pretend to knock it!

Shut the lavatory door!
                    (and lock it)

Conception

Thigh was like he was, hot, see?
not that he lusted after her
except in so far
as she
was coincident with that
hot thigh he got next to his
and did lust after

but with this difference, see?
that he did imply
he was commensurate with
the ingot he got close
to the pot of gold
in the clutch of her fair fat thighs

and so
this hobo got her down, see?
in the bare in the ditch
which the rain came down on
a light confetti
at her delicate, her spiderspun hairs
the wind raised

while the sun
a kite in the trees, see?
was strung there and stranded
as was she
in bright immoderate heats
the sun winked at
the twigs cracked at
my father hacked at
her belly tilted to receive me

Beware of the Boarhunt

Don't get in the way of the boarhunt
Or you'll be tortured to death
A Churchill tank will tumble along
And knock out yr teeth /

> Keep them, Honey
> You'll need them, Sonny
> To wrap round yr bread
> Don't tell them you dream
> Once you're in bed!

I dreamed last night I was walking
(after a lightgreen rain)
hand in hand with a little girl
her breasts exposed to the moon
A brand she held in her hand,
snakes of vermilion fire
When the flames had died
I took her for my lyre,
Her skin smelled of blown roses
springwarm on her sapling skin
"I came to pray for rain," she said
Her eyes were green, deep green
At last we walked up the sky
along the Milky Way
round Orion's studded belt
where flame of novas play
I kissed her for the last time
on each green-tinted breast
She walked out across the void
as the sun rose from the west…

So don't get in the way of the boarhunt
Don't get run over by a tank
Or you'll never walk with a shy young girl
& you'll end up in a bank.

Marilyn

On her, a soft and secret cunt
attention wets his lips;
amazing sweet the taste of her
and firm and sprung the waist of her
in my heart's wound she whets her spur
my life spurts into her belly's jar!

Marilyn,
my Indiana girl as rare as rare
that I might be where her haunches are
and eat her there as she eats her caviar!

Hairs on white wax like lashes lie
at the brink of an eye
and my luv's thrust nigh
the toss of her hips
whips my sperm to the sky
my balls in her hot nest of knowing!

What Is That?

Say: "I need love"/ but
what is that?

Superscope in an Homburg hat?

Intimate suck of a vampire bat?

A kiss, a fuck, a sly caress?

An all but lethal sabre's cut?

Indeed, for O in rut
the ultimate spasm was death

Sir Stephen said: *Yes* /   anus
of an angel, pefume of a slut / but
what is that?

They're all birds to a cat.

A Beginning

Naked
    is a beginning
that can
in man
or woman
strike a gazing face
like sunlight
or, if you have a dirty mind
like shite

Naked is
    bright, bright
    flesh
fresh as flowers
    flesh
as powers, towers
all mind of
our sure kind...

Sigma

sigmal vocab
sigmen
sigma $= 0 - \infty$, every individual
ONE
ALL,   not by birth or badge
nor necessarily thru evangelism of ours.
it is the secret history of the age
we plumb
in our dumb, slow way
starship textbook for today

A Prolegomena to Praxis

The printed matter
to effect contemporaries
in history
in lands and in lavatories
(that were my risk's
           laboratories)
must compete for tired
           attentions
in a mob, a tribe of
           regimented malcontents

A man invents

a man, alive
a man behind a face
which stops
like acid drops
quick tongues
           among factories and tents

the fiction, a function of facts
expressive of green power
transcends the perpetual friction
of Babel
the whole action
cast in the noble diction
           of revolt.

Warm blood, snake thrust, pure salt.

For John Donne
Master Metaphysical

Hear! this is what I
shall do to your body,
I shall play it as
a loved instrument
in touching it at deeps
touch you, my love
and gratify yr shyest intimations
of a perfect sexuality
in concrete terms
absorb at you
in me, round you
with all of spring & grass
our bright and coloured panoply!
Hear this: is what I
do to you. I mould
the very matter of yr
body's argument
a sweeter heroin
at yr crotch
to hard, my hot intent.
Take lips to suck
at short-haired places
still garlanded
with passion's traces

(Just a moment till
I undo my braces)

27

Fear

Where you have fear
you will have rot,
& rats of fear will run.

So
Build a broad stages
with many burrows off
into which the rats of fear may run.

Into My Church

Into my church wilt
thou come naked,
maidens and men...
On my altar
through red scar
will white sperm spurt
to ring loud
thy belly's jar!
And join loin
with bellies bare.
Teat, groin & spoor
In me so hard
My Koohinoor!

Into this room you walk naked
maidens and men
God's grace to "the wicked"
in our modern be-in.

The others are sick-led
from yesterday's midden...
to a heaven for helots
incompetently ridden.

Keep yr hell fr yr helots
& the other unfree
All flesh is fair
All flesh is for me
when flesh moves to flesh
like a young girl at prayer
I would be there...
would be & walk there.

End & Beginning

Everything moves towards
    the fall—& earth
    unconsciously attends
the waning embers of a
    distant fire
within earth moves
another being, becoming—
    evolt the lyre
whose strains may overtake
the parent sun
& plant a greater ore
in the cold belly of the
    Milky Way
The sperm is laid for that
    new day
on what fantastic world
when this earth's dead?

To give
To strive
and steer
sure as a Viking oar
To reach the core
of something more
than man
who could
no longer can
that race is run
and now: the sun
          or son
is all tomorrow's
    possibility
Visibility: excellent.

A *Little Geography Lesson for*
my Sons and Daughters

The east is onion-domes,
a bowl of plague, gossamer nets.
in black distance, out of rising dust,
it is black and white, and many shades
of brown, a camel, a fakir's hand,
moon-pale skin of a Turkish butt,
caravans, endless sand.

The east is a green crescent
or a round red ball;
it is always elliptical.
tiled mosques, music, mystic fires,
dark-blooded breasts of women
who are princesses or pariahs.

The wise men came from the east.
its wisdom is dried up,
a fig with its many seeds;
its sayings (deeds)
inscribed on tablets
endures as stone endures,
but they are not precisely statements;
they are elliptical as the thighs of its women.
consult the sufis, the masters of zen.
remember Li Po, Saladin.

The east is a great beast at bay
in the desert, a mongol caravan.
distances are far.
there is snow in China.
there is whiskey at Kandahar.

The west is electric trains
a brass figure on a cross and

31

supply & demand
profit & loss.   there is no prevailing
colour in the west
unless we speak of that dictated by Schiaparelli
and that is for spring or autumn only.

The west is neither sun nor moon.
it is an eagle or a lion
and it is orientated upwards
like the cathedral at Chartres
or the Empire State Building.
no one came from the west
because it wasn't invented
until Columbus sailed to India.
Here bee dragons, roote of mandrake...
some ever since have regarded
the whole damn thing as a mistake.

The west is trapezium or parallelogram
and meets at many points.
the wisdom of the west is geometrical;
at its best, precisely statement;
largely a question of semantics
since the metaphysical abatement.
in Rome, even Naples, they eat with knife and fork;
year round there is hashish & heroin in New York.

The east is ghettos,
narrow streets & a high birthrate.
it is the colour of semen and murder,
of love & hate;
the colour of hunger and industrial strikes,
& slow, over all, vultures tilt like kites.
it goes on and on,
women pounding clothes on stone,
old ways in old bitches;
it is act, cataract,
rags to rags, riches to riches.

It is a black cross and three brass balls;
it is diastole, intumescence,
like a tropical fungus,
the well-sucked teats of its women
who grow old bearing children.
the wisdom of the east
is contained in Sunday newspapers;
always sensational, never new.
sayings inscribed in the hard arteries
of a news editor, and will endure
as long as it pays to have hard arteries.

It is exclamatory as lovers pricked
out of the dark by a policeman's torch.
it is the spawn of a fish,
a queue for the dole, diastole.
there are diamonds in Limehouse
fine lingerie in Harlem.

The west is boudoirs and actresses
and a dwindling aristocracy.
there is no prevailing colour in the west
unless it's the colour of yr money.
that, being largely a question of semen & silk,
it is sometimes necessary to resort to murder,
but it is called manslaughter.
it is a well-known trademark or a school blazer.

The west is systole, attenuation,
a properly modulated voice,
too much flesh drawn (by choice)
tight in a corset.
the wisdom of the west is a book of rules
not quite indispensable
for those who travel by Pullman.
Fortunately the women of the west
pivot on a more vital fulcrum,
take off their rules with their clothes,
are fond of orchids, imaginative in their discretion.

33

The west is a Daimler sports
driven by a negro in a white uniform.
it is Hamlet, King Lear.
there is prostitution in Boston,
abomination in Saint Cyr.

The east is a dark uterus,
darker than the waters of the Nile or the Euphrates.
she is female & her spawn
is a seeping alluvial silt, waiting
for the dredgers of the west, who is male,
an iron plough
for the soft black earth of the east.

If you will turn to page 11 of yr geography books
you will see that where east meets west
there is a spiney ridge of high mountains
which runs north and south
like a Great Wall of China.
according to geologists, this formidable barrier
(bigger than an aircraft carrier)
came into being fortuitously
by fission or eruption in prehistoric times.
that is not true, children, it was erected
by yr grandfather's father (an evil old man),
a device to get that same old sod elected
on a platform that undertook to prevent
our western races from being "infected"
by the smelly rabble
which collected near the Tower of Babel
to pray to other gods.

If there is anything that isn't clear
I refer you to the chronicles of Zarathustra
or to the *chieh-hein* of the Llama Swingitup.
if you can't get hold of these,
see me, please.
in N. Y., Shanghai

Paris or either of the Venices
London, Moscow, or Kabul
For years I had few appendices
as the empire the emperor
the court, the fool,
I am normally to be found
on unhallowed ground
where they last buried me,
or, if I am still quick,
not walking the deadman's halls,
you'll find me in the red light district
engraving koans on lavatory walls.

Understand, children, I am not preaching peace.
I am not preaching moderation.
goodnight sweet children, goodnight, goodnight!

"How at Thebes Tiresias, the Prophet, Told..."

I

How at Thebes Tiresias, the prophet,
                told
of many things, of gods, of men, of gold
                and, seeing all, saw
nothing, no thing entire of rhythm
                him
was no thing vermilion for in past days

how the Khazar, ten years fled
                was torn bloody
from bed
from (the unhaired thighs of)
the youngest daughter of Pepi
                the Assyrian
and butchered in proper time
                he
who a decade lord absolute was
                was
prëordained, the mob's victim

how consuls were broken on the red horn
                of the land, and
women of that country
considered their broken rumps
under a froth of Vandals
(such things resilient as corn
                all gold in wind
are seldom ruined...)

how, in the *donjon*, a poet sang
                of the rose
(with words I thee oppose)

brought dire judgement upon himself
of inquisition
and burned, one
        of many little fires
all honour to the Virgin

again, history comes scratching in
thief of illusion
(the rat in the gutter,
        the maggot in the butter
...ever the utter utterer)
it is raining and the naked lady
        in the *rue Jacob*
has closed a shutter
        on her sweet immodesties
and I would be where that dark body lies
(*combine j'aurais' voulu*
me radiner vers toi,   tout nu
        touts nus
        blanc zulu

twenty-five years have passed through me
        a long disease
I will not sell you indulgencies
        persists a small smell of dying
        in Madrid
still
in Escorial
an old woman fingers her beads

I am of a northern country
mixed bloods, race wars, brute memories
remembering former scars, drums
        on my green seas, destinies
I am of a northern country
        and sell no indulgencies

Life is a good thing
        grass, quick clean girls

lithe limbs for hot fucking
                    death has no beauty
at soft young mouths plucking
the breath that explodes in love
when young cunts get cocking

II

Between dead things is no communion
                    no history, no music
                    no making of children.
Shall I tell you history was written
                    on a woman's flanks
when Finn wrote himself into the blonde flands
                    of Hildeburgh, into Icarus?

It is seldom chronicled in the chronicles
                    of academic historians
who tell of begetting only as seen decisive
                    in the coins of nations
& yesterday a product of whose frustrations?
This man was courtier
                    in the court of an usurper.
Weep ye for Richard
weep ye for the fallen Plantagenet!

A certain edict was signed cementing a privilege,
& revoked by him, John, the Black, late returned
out of Tartary (he thought himself impaired).
It was written thus in the manuscripts
by a worthy scholar of Oxenford, master of ellipse
apostrophae, descriptiones, exempla, versed in
                    propriety
                    astrology
                    anatomy
                    alchemy
                    & ignorant

of a sinister potion drunk by the Black Duke
in a woman's tent in Tartar country.
Before his execution
a hammering of carpenters in a public place
(he wld be borne by mercenaries)
he called for ink and quills
and wrote three letters:

Epistola prima: to his wife, to bid her be calm
                   accept royal judgement
                   a question of degree
                   even as he accepted it
                   & wld comport himself
                   in death as in life
                   as did his grandfather.
                   —for Madeleine, his sympathy.
          item: that she shld protect Harolde, their
                   firstborn from ill humours and evil
                   companions
          item: that for seeming time she shld be chaste
                   unto his memorie
                   respecting the sacrament
                   with fit lament.

Epistola secunda: to God, was written
                   after the manner of confessions
                   of lusts, whores, bawds, prurience
                   necromantic practices
                   all manner of adulteries
                   nightly iniquities
as confessed by John, of the Duchy of Lancaster,
the Black, who followed the moon
in unhallowed places/ whose soule
Jesu Crist have mercie. Amen.

Epistola tertia: to a woman unknown, he caused
                   to be carried beyond the seas
                   beyond the mountains of Pamir

        by a trusted messenger
        slant eyes to read of treachery
    of an uncouth king, an usurper,
& of the death of the Black Duke at the hands of his
enemies.

Shall I tell you, Achmet, history
is hungry at a woman's loins?

III

There was one, Falstaff, a gentle knight of England…

Ho then Harry, thou mincing hound!
must thou swear thus
    tear thus at all my tapestries?
Dost thou think I paint with my foot, all allegro?
    a forked lightning?
Because thou com'st creeping
from the strong cream gut of Bella Forbes
all wet with woman's parts, wild wombwaters
God man! dost thou think to say
    howl all hell down on my tapestries!

Because two farts maketh no poem
Dost thou think two bellies cannot?

Have at thee hairs, Harry!
Dost think her amulet did not growl at thee?
was't not articulate?
was not her gut open like Christ's own wound
    a dark firmament?
Ay, and a lute too that played for thee!
Where's thy resilience?
The sweat of it! was there not shock sigh song enough
for Orpheus himself?
    Bella's wars, Harry

    bella's wars...
Wer't thou not weaned that thy wick's so wordless?
    bella's wars, ay
and known more wars in that vast vagina of hers
than candles been lit for the Virgin.
    Dost thou question her techniques
    her tupturtling
    her shinplay juberoll and abdominal shudders?
Gob!
What's poetry but such an intricate reaction?
Where's such poetry in all my tapestries?

Did'st know old Gaunt who had his crop clipped?
    a very plough!
    turned back more earth
earthed more urns than the Ram himself!
Where did'st thou think he learned his wars
    from his duty captain?
God knows some say so, boy, it's said in court
    a sad clout to his memory
Not a whisper, boy, of a tent in Tartary...
Thou remin'st me of the tent-weaver
he made a rattle of Christ's bones
    and drew the juice from mangoes,
    trees? they're curs'd for Christ that staked him—
fie, Hal, fie on thee unicorn!
will ye shave the lion and call it Purity?

I heard a song once, Hal
'twas very neatly turned as I remember
sung by a hotsweet wench with black hair
black eyes'd unfrock the Pope, near gave us a gravel!
a most admirable and winsome dialectic!

        Light on her limbs who is not faithless,
            But tormenteth,
              Yet is some ease to sing;
           Sun, in your rising through the corn,

41

Let forsworn,
Thy yellow radiance be felt
Upon her skin;
And warm to melt her faithfulness,
In her sweet self.

Lay thou upon her bed vague moon
Nightbird, tune
On her whitening limbs
A thread of silver ravishment,
Who is intent
Her sleep before to see
Tho' carelessly
Arrayed to leave a shoulder bare;
Night's end, with her virginitie.

The very salamander, Hal
        I was as high as an ass's turd!
Absolute substance, say's I, nor man gainsaid me
such theological juice
did't sing for Aquinas or the good St. Bernard
would unheretic an heretic, ay, even me Hal!
though *I* light candles only to excavate my way
to the fourposter,
It's God's good work, say's I, spite of the bulls
        spite that learned prejudice
        concerning *amator ardentior*
God's good work, the very essence of religion,
of Ovid and Capellanus (Love's chaplain he was)—
but then she danced, Hal!
skirt flying and legs apart
        thine for the asking!
In all the world there's no such warm dichotomy!
        Another flagon, Hal
        for thy old friend,
'tis more exactly sustaining than pig's blood
they say the Devil rides to it in metamorphosis
and 'twas a succubus, young Meg says

who fathom'd her yesternight
How? said I
Fart, said she ('tis a vulgar thing, that Meg
born in a bawdyhouse,
I have it on capital information
'tis a surprise to me she changed her lodgings)
A goat? said I
Ay, Horn'd, said she, but none of thy fourlegg'd
variety with such a cod'spiece I thought I'd burst my
sides!
Such a tongue, Hal, such a tongue!
and so young, Hal!
I swear I don't know what the world's coming to...

For myself, and of conviction, Hal
I will take unto me only virgins
that their diurnal spoor be fresh and sweetsmelling
their softer parts immaculate as pomegranates
certainly at the solstices
and the heat of the sun being far off
I am not, to speak precisely, pole-axed by twin heats
into a tart's bed...

Old Hal, old...
forgive me if I talk too much
'tis my onlie vice, my addiction to metaphysics
my logos and lexikon,
but for an old man, Hal 'tis fitness,
justice, or, as Plato had it, DIKAIOSUNE

What?
Who?
Meg!
Me!   (Excuse me, Hal...)
Coming Meg?
Coming my chicken..."

IV

As the wounds of Naaman are red wounds
so also are roses red, redder than anemoni...
In orthodox theology, quoth our prelate
the Virgin must not be represented in bed,
animal parts,   heats,   pains,   sweats
parting no clay at the nativity of Our Lord.

Neither did the stars,   their constellations
            lunar asterisms,   catalytic affinities
dominate His coming in essence or in accident
            Who created them,   the which to be granted
whether thou followest in the elaboration
            of thy doctrine
            Champeaux or Abélard.

Chrétien,   on the contrary,   made religion
            out of his ladie
            (further confusing the issue)
bending knee to her nakedness as before a shrine
            belly-believing in spite
            of himself,   his nicetie,
& falling thus,   whether he knew it or nay
into Gnosticism, Catharism, in short, into heresie,
            the excess of his spirituality
            clima(c)ting in its antipode
(opposites implying each other, excess in man
or angel being treason, infidelity)
the rising fogs of lust ungoverned by Aristotle

the object of his true vision was occluded
            which error
            or false doctrine
            childe of jongleur
            & tombeor
led to the intrusion of the Rose into holy places
            hélas!

to the depiction in stained glass
    of the Virgin in bed at Chartres!
How at Carbonek the womb of the Mother asserted itself
        a root in wet ground
      a winter's crust broken in spring rain
        a Helenless faithful
      a faithful again demanding a Helenface
the vapours of an equivocal ladie descended on the chalices
      and 3-in-1
      were 4
      & more, shades
of Olympus received ambiguous absolution
The prelates in solemn anxiety
        were hungry for someone to burn

    +

There was much burning in the city
the rites of plague and religion
all manner of terrible levers
For the conversion of foreigners
for the city's own.

If you had stood on a hill above the city
you would have seen many a small smoke
that was a burning man

    V

In the morning the moujiks
came down from high ground
bringing with them
white horses and brown horses
thongs of leather
come out of barren country
in heavy weather

from stony ground through low cloud
into green land

With them were no women
only memories
of broken hearths and high cloud
and racing moon
and dead things and icy water.
Down they came into southern lands
bearing black arrows for red slaughter.

(End of extant MS)

Tabula Rasa

To begin with: a *tabula rasa*
enter "I"
in sigmal, or metacategorical
posture
green is garden peas
& the leaves of trees,
the living stalk of youth
exudes a green juice
stains thigh
lean loin
white abdomen
a map of molecules, of i
    chor
    or
    (for) to seep
    deep dam
    of ham-
    merer Thor!
A second song of Maldoror?

To begin with
Continue with:
    a *tabula rasa*

The Man and the Moon

the night tinkles
a chromium cash register
the little balls are orderly in their slots
cats laugh, their pointed teeth
the Sisters of Mercy furl their nets

who can penetrate his own midnight?
laugh at his fear's blue algebra?
curb the insectal sputter of his own silences
while that great yellow gob, the moon
a jaundiced eye
shouts up at his shanks from the wet streets?

The Jolly Bishop

The son of God;
what a blessing
the secret wound
of guilt caressing
That's the salad
with proper dressing
for Calvary
is always pressing

Letters to Contemporaries

I

Tomorrow
March, 1964
I have dated things before
And will again
That commensurate with zen
And act as if
Except when
In zen
(Or dead?)
Go ahead
Assume I have the bread
Print it – tomorrow
Record it – tomorrow
Live it from now on
Use her phone
And his
The point is
Get it done
And once it is printed
Defend it against
Charges of obscenity
             sedition
             March
             April
             And May
I have luck
Brave women
and good companions.

II

November 10th, '69

Maurice, my dear, (as it were, on 2nd thoughts)
...for, of course, you are right to require
an immediate demonstration
of (by, with or from) "the sigmal equation"

And so, my letter
as we know, no better
artefact
all systems "go"
a futique today
is an antique tomorrow.

III

15 August, 1970

and so, dear Su
　　you see
i cannot lie
　　f'r where
wld the junkie b
　　without his Xmas tree?

i had it from
　　a little bird
a few past pecks
　　are now restored,
and as yr friend
　　is badly gored

but if you come
　　to see us soon
y'll skip on velvets
　　of the moon
& see how vast
　　phun city's grown...

IV

O tell me, Angel
exactly when
I can hash-cool
crash course in Zen
to suck at last
in bog or fen
that noticeable
disfigured wen?

And, tell me, Angel
is yr snatch
as gollywoggled a patch
as yr dark and tangled thatch?

O Caroline, O Caroline!
Wilt thou be mine
My heroin!
Allow me to press
my avid lips
twixt London's
swingingest of hips
and savour
angelsalt in sips!

Ah tell me, Angel,
where are found
the pillars of the underground?
And will they heed
the pibroch's sound
& each bind each around?

Tell me, girl –
for golden boy
is there death
or is there joy?

Did I Meet You in Persopolis?

When you speak of the "cannabis problem",
he sd then,
placing the wee green-
black ball of hashish
upon her gleam-
ing, creamsweet abdomen,
I take it you refer
to the garden of my uncle, the emir,
where the problem
is the manner in which you prefer
to absorb it...
the hashish, I mean,
tho she cld be more absorbing...
the problem too
to improve the quality
of hemp globally
& avoid fatuous remarks
& grim bulldog barks
abt something
of which you are ignorant...
& a matter of the most exquisite taste
in the tents of the black emir.

Did I meet you in Persopolis?

from *Sappho of Lesbos*

I

Ah, Sappho, let thy thighs in throttling
ecstasies of sense like jaws imprison me
and draw the tingling thread of ecstasy
about my loins; let posture like the cat
to watch with tensening of lips the prey
near bone-bared claws.

Your sweet cosmetic odours, the sacramental pigments
of your sulky loins, moist with the animal ichors
of your delicately false lust, the which without
poor innocence would make cattle of us all—

Ah, Sappho, let us know that two are two in all arithmetics,
that one is made in play most ritually kept
that cultivated forth the oils of ecstasy
in beehive state come softening identities away
transcendently, that there is surely love
in subjectivity. Ah, Sappho let thy thighs
in throttling jaws imprison me!

II

There is a pattern in our fates. Events recur.
The victim walks from chains to chains.

III

The spangled night has struck the sea with gold
embers of forgotten worlds. The prows of ships

shall cut it cleanly through and men shall sing
as Atthis dancing moves her slender hips
in riot dance to bring her lover to her from the sea.
The ancient gods of Greece will light her flashing
limbs, incite desire in the hearts of men.
Her wheeling midriff like the moon shall duly seeded
burst with fruit, figsweet and straight as men
who followed Saladin.

Lessons for Boys & Girls I

school leaving X cert., question 1

how large must
something b
2b obscene?

must tit b seen?
as big as body
or a butter bean?

can the queen bee
obscene?

is green clean?
an apple in a tub
on hallowe'en?

emerald or bean, green
even of a devil's thigh?

or like a lake
& steaming in a pigstye?
the eye that's green?

love fr a wench
spring-green...
know stench
b french
keep yr parties clean

fresh, as earth's green hair
but b ware
of clean sinners

god bless
obscene beginners
god bless the queen
& the haricot bean
all man
the fat & the lean
izza clean latrine
obscene?
a glowing belly's sheen?
or only in aberdeen?

grace b 4
dinner

notmeg b coz
she's thinner
4 supper, upper
undies dandy
4 d randy

&

if heard
can
obscenity b
inferred?

merde!

Lesson for Boys & Girls II

Concerning white geese of dover

now, the minister of aircraft production
the hon. john dracula
has just signed a contract fr a
progressive manufacture 'f
1,000 dreadnaught mk fck
tactical bombers
their eventual delivery
        "to procure
        peace"
        fr the geese
        in 1980

    &

in commending the governmental decision
brigadier general paralysis
        met with derision
        the vulgar ("commie") analysis
        such policy
        of necessity
        wld create
        the very bloody
        preconditions
        to obliterate
        the state—

        viz. corollaries
        fr where the dollar is
        binding contracts
        full employment

facts like cataracts
on a continuous nile
historical process
complex, but limited
as chess, mile after mile
spawning zombies
& factories fr
bigger and better bombies
implying continuation
gradual exacerbation
of absurd, ape-head
schisms

&

reality observed through victorian prisms
the world a circus of irreducible "isms"

&

strike fr the present
the anvil of thor
yr future is anchored
in the iron of war

here is the news:
at noon the brigadier expressed his views
that such theories
all ands, ifs & buts
were born of eggheads
no principles, no guts

meanwhile
trafalgar square
the view is 1st class
a strange fellow
howling prophecies
with nelson's column up his arse

as sporran implies kilt
near as Edinburgh 2 Leith
foreign policy implies
apes showing teeth
black ape-teeth
white ape-teeth
brown ape-teeth
yalar ape-teeth
gritting their prongs
all ape
all them aliens
sounding their gongs

so
the minister of aircraft production
the hon. john dracula
in placing a contract fr a
                    thousand dreadnaught
                    mk fck etcetera
moves massive industries into gear
                    and time locked
                    to the target year
                    & yes, they cld b there
                    all gleaming in the air

                    each quick mk fck
                    to melt a sitting duck
                    frm Delhi to Santander
                    & equipped with all
                    the latest appliances
                    to mend broken alliances
                    & fr the annihilation
                    of every goose and gander

                    black ape-teeth
                    white ape-teeth
                    brown ape-teeth

61

yalar ape-teeth
gritting their prongs
all ape, all teeth
imperialist devils
sounding their gongs

&

CRUNCH... greenpea soup?

the blood
the muck
the shite
which rivers here tonite!
atomic custard
hot as mustard
incinerating men
all manner of brains
& tripes
even the poor hypes being irradiated
gentlemen of the iridium-tipped
as well as
the non-tipped variety
endless cess-brown custard
that was society...

he shouts it out loud
take a look at that crowd
they're not happy
with this chappie

put a frame round 'im somebody
and sell the bastard!

then you want to be custard?
you choose
to do the Lambeth ooze?

the stuck up, low down cat
obscuring nelson's hat!
bloody foreigner
dirty rat
ratatatat!
yell, spit, hate
that's where they're at

what's he saying now?

Lessons for Boys & Girls III

And, by the way
from whom do banks obtain
the extraordinary gain
they sometimes condescend
to lend?
but not to you
my impecunious friend.

£ S D (*Love, Sex, Death Pounds,
Shillings, Pence Lysergic Acid*)

iron leaves glint,
where wind broke in,
red rot in rain
my death is lead,
cloven by slow,
radium-sharp shark-fin

in my soft tree-bole
bleeds pearl,
spreads spoor
of wee, unhungering,
ceaseless vole.

an end to blue and green
and tune;
no more delight
in the black cave
of yr feminine night.

the poor silt of my years
is thin to spread...
after I am dead, "Margarine,"
it will be said,
"he mistook it for butter."

and end to sun,
moon, sky,
no young girl now will lie
in hot halter
of a pregnancy.

...young witches,
old bitches,

silvered resilience
of stagelit thighs
hot, husky cries,
mascaraed eyes,
all manner of highs,
excruciatingly artificial.

few virtues,
threadbare ascription…
clues: blues
        cruise
        unpaid dues;
…dropped Plato
like a hot potato;
wouldn't work:
hashish of the Turk…

there was a door between
him and himself.
out, like the biff-ball
from the bat,
and limit taut,
feet sunk in cement,
tripped over himself,
a closing hinge:
himself something
upon which he couldn't impinge.

The Stinking Cauldron

The stinking cauldron
of inhibition soup
had its lid lifted
by Attacunt Peep
the hairy mind-wrestler
the child with which
god blessed her
womb, and the sweet lust
by which it was irradiated
in the hot pit
of her ecstasy-impregnated
    bed.

Let it be said
in Gath
that the daughters of the
philistines rejoice
at our coming
(our gentle thumbing
of their bodies' ready roses
our love imposes
on us, on them)
and their fathers be
    defeated.

+

And the weapons of war
    are perished.

The Worldly Wisdom of
Cdr T. Taskmaster Disaster, R. N.

Make sure all other ranks is now confined to camp
for don't you give the working classes rope
unless it's good old English hemp!
Otherwise, you'll find we cannot cope.
I'm not the bloody lady of the lamp!

A kick up the arse
a bob a tot of rum
that's good enough pickings
for you're A. B. English scum!

Fall'em in, fall'em out
or make'em work instead
set'em to chippin' paint
from the old bulkhead.

If it's raining weather
fall'em in upon the deck
complete with an unsoiled lanyard
around each bugger's neck!

Let the Bos'n call'em out
each bastard by his name
tell'em their tiddley titfers
are a crying bloody shame!

+

Make sure all other ranks is now confined to camp
Mustn't give the working classes rope
unless it's good old English hemp
from Lebanon…
They'll smoke it like the blacks

given half a chance
and then they'll learn to dance!
& say: "Me work?
        Go furk!"

In Pursuit of Woman

An age for each mood
Raw to seasoned wood
A lass at fifteen
fucks fine on the green
Put a spark to her fire
in a barn or a byre,
Like, after choir...

In bed a lass
is sweet at twenty
Come at her ten ways
rough & gently.

For golden thighs
and passion plenty
have you kissed her
elder sister?
A man for each
of her thrice-ten summers
have tongued their lust,
her body's drummers
her sinews long for
strident strummers!

And Venus is luscious
after forty:
"Right fit for kings"
her lust is courtly!

By now, you see, it
doesn't matter:
some are thin
others fatter

70

some women
are heaven
at seven
-ty. Fuck.
Good luck!

ADVT.

SITUATIONS: For whom the bell tolls,
What you want is always smthng
within a complex situation in (of)
present time.
We will provide the situation
without which what you desire
will remain a phantom...

the situation
the complex of
contents
or
conditns
the ions
the lions
reins of yr future
the suture
stopping the spill of blood.
The moment before the flood
of yr realization
you have at last
the secret of wanting.

S.A.E. for CONDITIONS—

Myrtle Again

Myrtle of the light blue hair
Myrtle of the body bare
Containing me within her snare
Moves like a turtle...
In Myrtle's thighs
my wet mouth cries
me lives, me dies...
this horse her cart fill.

L'Enfer... C'est les Autres: Views

my way is not the way of the Samsaras
to shake frail claws for bread
and spit on women.
i must walk in crowded places
until i am murdered by my own contempt.

+

the slack white body
of yr dead Aunt Peg
had a pink confection
for a face, the day
they buried her.

candy kisses
meet a dark stranger

+

– when i consider now
what happened then
oak, brass, and varnish
and a voice which said:
"Dear God, we thank thee
taking this Thy servant
unto Thy inscrutable comprehension!
for this cold seal Thou
settest on a broken breast,
our brother, the abelest."

gone in his prime
like yr gin and lime.

+

– that one was gassed in the
first world war on a
bleak field in Ghent
(or was it Gommorragh?)
anyway,
a redhot clamp at his lungs
suddenly, while sparrows
twittered and worms crawled.

other indistinguishable
crawl in him, completing
the cycle, bifurcating
his liver in divers ways.
victim of time
like yr gin and lime.

+

heehaw, heehaw, heehaw!
said the fire engine, in the night
a great hot electric mare
trumpetting her cold heat
through the quaking streets
an accident-stricken city.
heehaw, heehaw, heehaw!
said the fire engine, panic-bright!

there, among the swarm of peopled rooms
drawn blinds, in prurient-sweet secrecy
a living object
with fair, flat slabs of fresh flesh
warm and desiring, hairsoft and damp
jungles at her sweet, her admirable crotch

21

Into this room you walk
naked maidens, naked men
God's grace to "wickedness"
in our communal be-in.

All the others sick-led
from yesterday's midden—
to a heaven for helots
incompetently ridden.

Keep yr hell fr yr helots
& others unfree
All flesh debonair
and fair is for me
when flesh moves to flesh
like a young girl at prayer
in the flesh, in the hair
then would i be there...

Boxes...

Place prime ministers upon cruisers
& rendezvous off Cap Ferrat
let them come upon a solution
or drown where they're bloody at.

Snap
& so you tried to get it
down. *Her nickerstrap?*
No. In words I mean. *What?*
This. *That claptrap?*

a round ring
for a love
any bloody thing
at all
that makes penetration
deaeper
& ecstasy in a belly, in a ball
and that is truth withal

In my words
do linger
fingers there

When the spirit of play dies
there is only murder
When the flesh is hypocrite
there is only war

Things is nice scented
unless y're a puritan
& pee in a can

General Apathy,
after apoplexy, frowned;
had caught a chill on enemy ground;
pneumonia/the general drowned.

It's called the "fold-in"
method
But, when pressed
my wise friend B
was at pains to insist
he "chews" before folding

Man at Leisure

                    his world picture was
                    his word picture and
                    his vocabulary, obscene

The first duty of a
        young man
without private means
is, as soon as he can
be paid for heart loved leisure
his can of beans
and walk with his head
in the posture of queens

Men who work
in the conventional sense
of the word
are bad at furk
& fr purposes of identity
might wear rings in
        thr noses
might have been born
at the time of Moses

                +

A jerk, it is
claims the "right to work"
not I
said Cockrobin
to his oulde friend Dobbin
but how to get
one's equitable share
of the national product

(BY RIGHT OF INHERITANCE)
& dance
& woe betide
who brushes me aside

And so, sd Cockrobin:
The "right to work"
is for the birds
one of the turds
I can do without
GIVE IT TO THE WORKING CLASS
wherever it's foolish enough to be.

America

Breast culture
Land of mothers' sons
For cunt
Use deodorunt
For pricks
Kleenix

Sexistential...

                    Man at work
                    FOR EXPORT.
Slid in her carport, contrapuntally
slithering...
Contraception good: DAILY EXPRESS
                    CRASHES AT
                    LAST CROSSING
Man at leisure:
            a long, long day
            which oughtn't necessarily
            to end in 24 hours
            can a biological necessity
            destroy a bank holiday
            or to think of living necessarily
            in 24 hour cycles ---
            they will call it a biological
            necessity
            You wld destroy a Bank Holiday?

Afterword

A LEX TROCCHI'S GROWING REPUTATION in literary circles has to date been based almost exclusively on his prose. On one level this is not surprising, since the verse collected in this book is of variable quality. That said, Trocchi's initial impact and enduring appeal are grounded as much in his personality and "legend" as his actual writing; when looking at Trocchi from non-literary perspectives, his poetry is in many ways more significant than his fiction.

Trocchi's commitment to poetry is readily evident from Jamie Wadhawan's 1969 documentary *Cain's Film*. This begins with Trocchi trying to persuade his publisher to take a collection of his verse, only to be rebuffed by Marion Boyars, who tells him that poetry doesn't sell. Trocchi persisted and John Calder issued *Man At Leisure* just three years later (despite the views of his business partner at Calder & Boyars). Returning briefly to *Cain's Film,* this more or less concludes with Trocchi reading the poem *Lessons Fr Boys & Girls II* at the Arts Lab in London's Covent Garden on 13th April 1969. Wadhawan's portrait of Trocchi is thus framed to emphasize the fact that he is above all else a poet.

Slightly earlier in his anti-career, Trocchi acted as MC at the *International Poetry Incarnation* AKA *Wholly Communion* at The Albert Hall. To some this marked the last and greatest hurrah of the London beatnik scene, to others it signified the birth of hippy culture. That said, for the several thousand punters who turned up to witness the event on 11th June 1965, *Wholly Communion* was a spectacular success. The individual poetry readings were less inspiring than the sum total of their overall effect, since even the appearance by beat stalwart Allen Ginsberg was viewed by many as disappointing. Regardless, Trocchi was at the very centre of the action and kept things moving with off-the-cuff comments about getting a few poets together and allowing them to "act naturally".

In an essay about Trocchi, *Lord Junk Himself*, Denis Browne recounts meeting his literary idol through an uncle who ran a bar in Kensington, west London. The publican was presented with a copy of *Man At Leisure*, but since he wasn't interested in modern poetry, Browne ended up with both the book and an honorary job as Trocchi's literary assistant. Trocchi liked to surround himself with people who dug poetry. Hipsters on the beatnik scene held poets in the kind of esteem that later generations accorded to rock stars. In London, Trocchi's immediate circle consisted almost exclusively of individuals who'd transformed drug addiction into a kind of poetry, and a dude known as Grainger was one of the most notable among them.

Grainger had suffered what was probably his first bust in the spring of 1962. This led to the headline "5 Idle Chelsea Men Had Hemp" in *The Times* of 24th April that year. Grainger was tried under his legal name of Malcolm Drake; like those arraigned with him, he was unemployed. After he was informed that Grainger aspired to being a poet, the magistrate announced: "That is a nice job for the evenings and getting up in the morning to see the sun rise." The beak was not impressed with the defendants "long hair" and seems to have viewed them all as worse than work-shy, ranting after reading a report on Grainger's flatmate John Beaumont that: "...your philosophy is that work has to be avoided at all costs. You have almost a religious faith in being able to exist without earning any money..." From this it can be seen that Trocchi's inner circle thought and behaved pretty much as he did. By the late-Sixties, Grainger and Trocchi saw themselves as individuals who lived poetically, and therefore didn't need to write.

The Situationist International, of which Trocchi had been a founding member in 1957, understood revolutionary activity itself to be a form of poetry. Raoul Vaneigem states in *The Revolution of Everyday Life* (Rebel Press & Left Bank Books,

1983, page 153) that: "Poetry is... 'making' but 'making' restored to the purity of its moment of genesis – seen, in other words, from the point of view of the totality." Likewise, among the most famous Situationist slogans is one that runs: "Never Work". The Situationists, like Trocchi, gave themselves over to an art of living that was in itself poetic.

Trocchi's poetry is thus central to any rounded understanding of both him and his immediate scene. This alone would make the pieces in this book worth reading. But beyond this they are enjoyable in themselves; sometimes they reveal real flashes of insight, and at others they work more on the level of verse that is so bad it is good. Trocchi is very much about peaks and troughs, and that shouldn't surprise anyone who understands that he self-consciously rejected the bourgeois literary compromises associated with evenness of tone and "quality".

– Stewart Home
April 2009

ONEWORLD CLASSICS

ONEWORLD CLASSICS aims to publish mainstream and lesser-known European classics in an innovative and striking way, while employing the highest editorial and production standards. By way of a unique approach the range offers much more, both visually and textually, than readers have come to expect from contemporary classics publishing.

∾

GIUSEPPE GIOACCHINO BELLI: *Sonnets*
Translated by Mike Stocks

GIACOMO LEOPARDI: *Canti*
Translated by J.G. Nichols

DANTE ALIGHIERI: *Rime*
Translated by Anthony Mortimer and J.G. Nichols

BOILEAU: *The Art of Poetry* and *Lutrin*
Translated by William Soames and John Ozell

The Song of Igor's Campaign
Translated by Brian Reeve

CECCO ANGIOLIERI: *Sonnets*
Translated by C.H. Scott

POPE: *The Art of Sinking in Poetry*

ERICH FRIED: *100 Poems without a Country*

ERICH FRIED: *Love Poems*